INVENTORS & INVENTIONS

AIRPLANES

INVENTORS & INVENTIONS

AIRPLANES

GINI HOLLAND

BENCHMARK BOOKS

MARSHALL CAVENDISH
NEW YORK

Benchmark Books
Marshall Cavendish Corporation
99 White Plains Road
Tarrytown, New York 10591-9001

©Marshall Cavendish Corporation, 1996

Series created by The Creative Publishing Company

Library of Congress Cataloging-in-Publication Data

Holland, Gini.
    Airplanes / Gini Holland.
        p.   cm. -- (Inventors & inventions)
    Includes biographical references and index.
    Summary: Covers the history and future of aviation and includes
discussions of different types of planes and how they work.
    ISBN 0-7614-0068-0
    1. Airplanes--Juvenile literature.   [1. Airplanes.]   I. Holland,
Gini.   II. Title.   III. Series.
TL547.F628   1995
629.133'34--dc20

                                               95-9099
                                                 CIP
                                                     AC

Printed and bound in Hong Kong

Acknowledgments

Technical Consultant: Teodoro C. Robles, Ph.D.
Illustrations on pages 36 and 41 by Julian Baker

The publishers would like to thank the following for their permission to reproduce photographs:
Austin J. Brown/Aviation Picture Library, (21, 25, 29, 34, 46, 50, 52, 54); Eye Ubiquitous, (Tim Page 30); Peter Newark's Historical Pictures, (8); Peter Newark's Military Pictures, (12, 22, 27, 45); Quadrant, (7, 9, 20, 28, 38, 39, 48, 53); Science Photo Library Ltd., (Peter Menzel front cover, NASA frontispiece, U.S. Library of Congress 11, Dick Luria 42, Peter Menzel 43, NASA 49, 57, Lawrence Livermore National Laboratory 59); UPI/Bettmann, (10, 15, 16, 18, 19, 24, 32, 33, 56).

(Cover) Ground crew at Edwards Air Force Base, California, tend a Rockwell B-1 bomber.

(Frontispiece) A Lockheed SR-71 aircraft approaches the boom of a KC-135 tanker for in-flight refueling.

Contents

Chapter 1
First Flights

AMAZING FACTS

The completed X-1 was nearly 11 feet (3.4 meters) high, almost 31 feet (9.5 meters) long, and had a wingspan of 28 feet (8.5 meters), but the pilot had a very small cockpit crammed with recording instruments. Fuel took up a lot of room. The 465 gallons (1,762 liters) of liquid oxygen and 498 gallons (1,887 liters) of alcohol that fueled the plane were completely consumed in two and one-half minutes at full power.

The test pilot climbed high and, as he turned to dive, he wondered if he could still control his plane. When he approached the speed of sound, he felt his aircraft shake. He tried to move the controls, but they locked in place as he fell faster and faster toward Earth. He knew that others had crashed because they couldn't pull out in time, so he fought the controls and found they loosened up a bit at lower atmosphere levels. With relief, he felt the plane respond as he pulled it out of the dive.

He was one of the lucky ones. Others had died. One of his buddies said later it was like "trying to fly straw in a hurricane." Was the speed of sound a barrier preventing planes from going faster? Back in the 1940s, it certainly looked that way.

In World War II, the military forces of both sides wanted faster planes, but to break through the sound barrier, better controls and stronger planes were needed. Plane designers returned to their drafting boards. When they used wind tunnel tests they found that pressures around a plane peaked as air approached the speed of sound, battering the aircraft and locking controls in place. Some test planes just disintegrated. Other aircraft, mechanically controlled from the ground without a pilot, simply disappeared.

The problem was that at speeds above Mach .7 (roughly the speed of sound) the air molecules flowing over the wings compress, bunching together faster than they can move away from the airplane. This causes a shock wave of air molecules that hits control surfaces and fragile wing material, "freezing" controls and battering the wings.

In 1945, a group of U.S. engineers at Bell Aircraft thought of a creative way to solve this problem. They designed the rocket-powered X-1 plane in the shape of a .50 caliber bullet, since this ammunition had reached supersonic speeds (beyond the speed of sound). They made the plane of special aluminum that could withstand eighteen times the force of gravity pressing against it and gave it very thin wings to reduce the effect of air turbulence and shock waves.

Cracking Through the Sound Barrier

The U.S. Air Force took over this X-1 project in 1947. Of the eight or so test pilots that volunteered, Charles "Chuck" Yeager got the assignment.

Yeager put the X-1 (named the *Glamorous Glennis* after his wife) through increasingly difficult maneuvers. When he brought the plane close to the speed of sound, he hit the same barrier that had caused the deaths of other pilots. As his controls jammed, he shut off his rockets and let gravity reduce his speed, dragging him back to lower altitudes where he could again maneuver the plane.

Flight engineer Jack Ridley changed the design of the controls to stabilize the plane, so on October 14, 1947, Yeager climbed into the X-1 once more. "My heart was in my mouth and my stomach right behind it." He climbed to nearly eight miles (thirteen kilometers) above the ground, leveled off, refired one of his rockets, and noted that the pressures seemed to diminish the faster he went. His measure of speed, the Machmeter, moved

Chuck Yeager and Glamorous Glennis, in which he made the first supersonic flight. Many years later he said, "As the pilot I got a large share of the glory, but I can truly say it was a team effort to construct, instrument and fly the fifty X-1 flights that led to the conquest of the sound barrier."

+35364 A.C.

7

up to .965 and then jumped off the scale for eighteen seconds during which Yeager had a smooth ride. With a crack like thunder chasing behind him, he had broken the sound barrier with the first sustained flight that moved faster than the speed of sound. He had opened the way for supersonic flight.

How Flight Began

When you see planes landing at a busy airport, it's hard to remember that this invention first succeeded back on December 17, 1903, close to one hundred years ago. Over the many centuries before this date, people in all cultures had dreamed of flying. The ancient Greeks had told stories of men flying too close to the sun, and the Chinese had legends of kites that carried people skyward. Chinese acrobats even used small parachutes in their acts to amuse their audiences as they tumbled. In the 1500s, Italian artist and inventor Leonardo da Vinci drew the designs of an airplane, a parachute, and even a helicopter, which he called an "air-screw." In 1709, Bartolomeu de Gusamo, a Brazilian priest, showed off an unpiloted hot air balloon for King John V of Portugal.

As the airplane captured the public's attention, new ideas were tried. The monoplane, with a single wing instead of the double wing the Wright brothers used, was the creation of Louis Blériot. He crossed the English Channel, flying from France to England, in his Blériot XI in 1909.

Many people attempted to fly before the Wright brothers succeeded in 1903 with the first powered, controlled flight. That day, Orville and Wilbur Wright, taking turns on their plane, *The Flyer*, were able to achieve a record, staying up fifty-nine seconds to travel 852 feet (260 meters) over Kitty Hawk, North Carolina, at a poky speed of less than seven miles per hour (eleven kilometers per hour).

It took only three years after the success of the Wright brothers for the first recorded speed record to be entered in the books. People in Europe began building airplanes and holding air races, and Alberto Santos-

Harriet Quimby was the first woman to become a licensed pilot in the U.S. and became the first woman to pilot an airplane from England to France in April 1912.

Dumont, a Brazilian, flew his biplane at 25.65 miles per hour (41.3 kilometers per hour) on November 12, 1906. However, the Americans were not to be outdone. In 1908, the Wright brothers brought their *Wright Flyer* to France and broke the 100-kilometer (62-mile) mark with a flight of 120 kilometers (74.5 miles) in just one hour and fifty-four minutes, or about 37 miles per hour (60 kilometers per hour). These brothers had certainly improved their plane's speed and distance in just five years!

Some of the early daredevils such as Lincoln Beachey, Charles Willard, and Harriet Quimby performed acrobatic maneuvers with their planes before crowds of astonished admirers. Stunts included wing-walking, planes doing airborne somersaults, and pilots in open cockpits who flew upside down. To add to their drama, wing walkers and pilots often wore long scarves that streaked straight behind them during flight.

AMAZING FACTS

Before there were airplanes, there were gliders. Sir George Cayley built the first one in 1809, but it wasn't until 1856 that a Frenchman, Jean-Marie Le Bris, made the first actual flight in one.

Orville Wright (1871–1948) and Wilbur Wright (1867–1912)

While these two brothers are famous for their motor-powered flight at Kitty Hawk, North Carolina, in 1903, perhaps they made an even greater discovery the year before. In 1902, they studied how to keep a plane stable and how to make it turn when and where they wanted it to go. When they mounted the engine in their craft in 1903, they had the means of guiding the plane.

As children, the brothers loved mechanical things. It was said that they had inherited their mechanical genius from their mother, Susan Koerner Wright. She was always inventing new kitchen utensils and could mend anything broken.

In their home workshop, the brothers built a printing press and published a four-page weekly newspaper. Then, they branched out into bicycles and founded a profitable business in 1892.

Four years later, the brothers became interested in gliders. First, the Wrights experimented with kites and then, in 1899, built their first glider for fifteen dollars. Wilbur made the wings control the movement of the plane.

They tried their new system with two planes. While the controls were fine, they still had problems lifting the plane off the ground and decided they needed more accurate scientific information. They built themselves a crude, small wind tunnel in which they tested more than two hundred shapes and sizes of wings. Finally, the Wrights had a glider that performed satisfactorily.

Now, they needed an engine. The brothers rebuilt an automobile engine, substituting aluminum parts for the heavier steel ones. They made their propeller of wood, using the information they had gleaned from their wind tunnel experiments. The plane had no

Wilbur, left, and Orville Wright in 1909.

wheels but rather skids, like a sled, that rested on a greased sheet-iron strip the craft would travel along before lifting into the air.

Wilbur won the toss of a coin to see who would have the first chance to try the machine. The plane was in the air only seconds before it crashed. After three days for repairs, on December 17, 1903, Orville took the next try, and though the flight was only twelve seconds long and covered 120 feet (37 meters), it was the first time that a machine with a man had, by its own power, flown in the air without reduction of speed and had landed at a point as high as that on takeoff. Finally, Wilbur took the plane up for 59 seconds and a distance of 852 feet (260 meters). Then, a gust of wind turned the machine over, causing damages that ended any more attempts that year.

The Wrights went on perfecting their machine. However, the American public and government did not show much interest in their invention. The Europeans responded with more enthusiasm when the Wrights demonstrated their plane in France in 1908.

Wilbur died in 1912 of typhoid fever; Orville, in 1948. After Wilbur's death, Orville sold everything including his patents to some New York buyers and retired a wealthy man. The pioneering work of the Wright brothers in developing both the theory and the first machine for controlled, powered flight provided the basis for the development of the aircraft industry.

Planes in World War I

The military had already seen the potential of air observations by using balloons. Benjamin Franklin had written of the possibilities for military use of the balloons he witnessed when he was a diplomat in France, and balloons were used by both Union and Confederate forces in the American Civil War.

With World War I breaking out first in Europe in 1914, the airplane was used not only for observations but for bursting observation balloons, for bombing, for attacking submarines, and for fighting other planes in what came to be known as dogfights. At the beginning of the war, pilots (who had only a few hours of training before takeoff) found their planes unreliable, subject to breakdowns, and not performing as expected. However, designers came up with new planes that were more reliable, and ultimately as many as forty thousand pilots were involved on both sides of the war.

World War I gave the United States a great boost in the development of its aviation industry. When the United States entered the war in 1917, it had far fewer planes available for the military than did the countries of Europe, but it soon caught up. During the war, the United States trained thousands of workers in aircraft manufacturing. It applied the lessons learned from its automobile industry, where mass production, with parts that could be used on different models, made production easy. By the end of the war in 1918, the country was producing twelve hundred planes a year and thousands of pilots. The experience gained in these combat conditions promoted further development in peacetime, leading to the golden age of aviation.

This painting by Geoffrey Watson portrays the last flight of "The Red Baron," Manfred von Richthofen, in 1918. Richthofen was one of the most famous aces, or successful fighter pilots, in World War I. During the war, pilots also tried new tactics, such as formation flying as opposed to one-on-one fights, and learned to fight in teams, or squadrons.

Chapter 2
The Golden Age
of Aviation

With peacetime optimism, the public hailed aviation as a fresh, new field where a person could become famous by breaking flight records and rich by designing new planes. Airplanes were entering what has been called their "golden age."

Between World War I and the beginning of World War II in 1939, inventors came up with new planes and new uses for them, including the first modern airliner, United Airlines's Boeing 247. Made entirely of metal in a revolutionary design, it took off for the first time in the United States in March 1933. It could carry only ten passengers, the most the designers thought would want to fly at one time! The 247's first flight crossed the United States in under twenty hours, passing through four time zones in less than a day. An aircraft with wings placed low on its body and twin engines, it came equipped with retractable landing gear, wing deicers, constant-speed (similar to cruise control in a car), and designed to let an automatic pilot mechanism take over when needed. Best of all, it could fly on a single engine if it had to — a good safety feature. Seeing its immediate appeal for passenger service, United Airlines promptly bought the first sixty produced.

Development of the Airline Industry

Because of the size of the United States, air travel required covering great distances. Europe, with its shorter hops between countries, at first had the advantage in air travel because the early planes matched Western Europe's need for short-distance connections. The railway system in the United States looked like a better way to serve U.S. transportation needs. However, with the bigger and better planes built in the 1920s, the United States was a perfect market. America's huge size meant it could use fast, long-distance transportation to improve travel within the country. Also, it had a large middle class that could afford this new form of passenger service.

Seeing the possibility of customers anxious to climb on board, Transcontinental & World Airlines (TWA) asked Douglas Aircraft to design a plane for them. By 1936, the DC-3 was created; it could carry twenty-one passengers and make a profit on its flight without having to carry mail, unlike earlier planes.

New Heroes

Pilots became the heroes and heroines of the day. One of the most glamorous professions was ferrying mail by plane. Coast-to-coast airmail had been established in 1918, but in 1925, the government decided to transfer the service to private companies that bid for the jobs. This kind of cooperation between government and private industry helped stimulate the growth of the country's air industry.

Charles Lindbergh was one of these experienced airmail pilots, and he wanted to fly the best equipment available. When he heard of an improvement over the liquid-cooled engines that were used during World War I, he wanted the new air-cooled radial engine. Made by the Wright Aeronautical Corporation, it appeared more reliable and required less maintenance than earlier engines. So Lindbergh went to the Ryan Company of San Diego, where he designed and built an airplane with this new engine. He called his plane the *Spirit of St. Louis*. When someone offered a prize of $25,000 to the first person to fly nonstop between New York and Paris, France, Lindbergh was ready to meet the challenge.

Seventy-eight people had already crossed the Atlantic in airplanes, but Lindbergh was the first one to do it alone, with an amazing nonstop flight between North America and the mainland of Europe.

New Records and Experiments

Meanwhile, air shows around the country continued to popularize this new means of transportation. Pilots, such as Bessie Coleman, who was the first African-American woman to get a license, treated small communities to the excitement of flight. Air races for the Bendix and Thompson trophies established Jimmy Doolittle and Roscoe Turner as heroes. New records for speed, height, distance, and new routes made names for many, among them Howard Hughes, Wiley Post, Richard E. Byrd, Amy Johnson, and Amelia Earhart.

Bessie Coleman (1892–1926)

Bessie Coleman had two strikes against her flying when she was born in 1892 in Atlanta, Texas. She was female and she was black. Moreover, her family objected to the idea of her flying.

She was born in a one-room cabin, raised in a single parent family, and attended a school for black children. It is likely that her mother was born a slave, but her father may have been free, with three of his grandparents probably Choctaw or Cherokee Indians. Neither

parent knew how to read or write, but her mother encouraged Bessie to dream and to amount to something: "You can't make a race horse out of a mule. If you stay a mule, you'll never win the race."

Coleman picked cotton to earn money for college. After one semester, she was out of money and moved north with her family. In Chicago, she worked in a beauty parlor and a restaurant, married, and watched her two brothers go off to war. When brother John returned, he teased Bessie that French women were better than those on Chicago's South Side. The French women had careers. They even flew airplanes.

Coleman decided that by flying, she would amount to something. No flight schools in the United States would accept African-American students, so she studied French and went off to France for flying lessons. Robert Abbott, the editor and publisher of the *Chicago Defender,* backed her.

In France, Coleman's room was nine miles (14.5 kilometers) from the airfield. She walked it every day for ten months. She earned her pilot's license in 1921 and then returned to the United States where she hoped to earn money as a stunt pilot. She was met by reporters who praised her achievement.

Coleman wanted to start a school for black pilots and had saved almost enough to achieve this. She said she hoped to "give a little coloring" to aviation; "the air is the only place free from prejudices."

Large crowds gathered to watch her performances at flying exhibitions. However, she was killed in 1926 while practicing stunts with someone else at the controls of the plane.

Dr. Mae Jemison, the first African-American female astronaut, said of the frequent comparisons of her with Coleman: "On the surface folks could say we were both young black women born in the South who lived in Chicago and became involved in science and technology fields — aviation and aerospace — when women and especially black women whether through commission or omission were traditionally kept from participation. One could speak of the lack of role models and facing adversity. It is easy to get caught up in the airplane, mechanical, flyboy stuff. But what I hope is common to me and Bessie is the smile of adventure, self-determination, and dogged will to see beauty in the world even as ugly things happen around us and to us."

No longer at war, governments of the countries leading in aviation did not spend much on military planes until 1935. However, most of these governments continued to pursue research and airplane development in case of war. Moreover, they shared their information with private companies and gave support to those who built planes for use in commercial flight. Soon, civilian planes were winning more speed races than military planes. This was because of inventors like Walter Beech, who built the first plane with an air-cooled radial engine that could fly faster than 200 miles per hour (322 kilometers per hour).

First trying to fly like birds, pilots were now able to zip past them with ever-improving technology. Fred Weick, Frank Caldwell, and James Doolittle all made improvements in the way airplanes worked, while Howard Hughes built his H-1 Racer, considered one of the most beautiful piston-engine planes. William Piper and C. G. Taylor designed and manufactured Piper Cubs, light planes for civilian pilots that helped make aviation a thrilling, if somewhat dangerous, hobby.

People tried new kinds of air travel, including dirigibles, those hydrogen gas-filled balloons (often called airships) that are propeller-driven and have room underneath for passengers, crew, and cargo. Dirigibles were supposed to compete with ocean liners. However, the risk of explosion was great because the hydrogen gas that made the dirigible lighter than air catches fire easily. In 1937, an explosion wrecked the German *Hindenburg* dirigible in New Jersey and terrified its crew and passengers in a violent firestorm that killed

The German airship Hindenburg *explodes in New Jersey on May 6, 1937. This tragedy caused dirigibles filled with hydrogen gas to be abandoned in favor of safer means of transportation.*

thirty-six of the ninety-seven people on board. The public saw how frightening and dangerous airships could be.

Seaplanes, equipped with floats in place of wheels so they could land on water, dominated this period on overwater routes.

At the time of its first flight in 1939, the Yankee Clipper was the largest plane in the world. Seaplanes continued in popular use during World War II. However, with the wartime increase in airport construction throughout the world and with improvements in four-engine land aircraft, the use of seaplanes diminished.

Landing on water was easier and less expensive than building airports, and people felt safer flying over oceans when they knew they could make an emergency landing without sinking. Seaplanes such as Pan American's Sikorsky and Boeing Clippers brought passengers the first regular transoceanic routes. Igor Sikorsky was one of the pioneers in the design of seaplanes, but he is probably best known for his development of the helicopter, which he flew in 1939. However, even earlier, back in 1913, he built the first four-engine plane, Le Grand, for the Russian army.

Igor Sikorsky (1889–1972)

Igor Sikorsky was a "triple-threat inventor," giving aviation the multi-motored airplane, the big flying boats, and the helicopter. He was born in Kiev, Ukraine, in 1889. His father was a physician and professor of psychology. His mother was also a physician but never practiced. However, she had a great interest in the life of Leonardo da Vinci, who had sketched ideas for flight in 1500. Perhaps her interest affected her son, who, at the age of twelve, made a small model helicopter powered by a rubber band.

In 1903, Sikorsky became a student at the Russian Naval Academy, but he resigned from the service in 1906 to pursue an interest in engineering. On a trip in Europe in 1908, he heard of the work of the Wright brothers and of the European plane designers. He decided to investigate vertical take-off flight. The following year, he constructed a helicopter that did not fly successfully. After another failure, he decided that he lacked the right materials, the money, and the experience for that project, so he set it aside.

By 1910, Sikorsky had built his first biplane and was able to make short cross-country flights by 1911. Then, he began to supply planes for the Russian army. By 1913, he had developed the first four-engined plane, Le Grand; with an enclosed cabin, it was far ahead of its time.

The Russian Revolution and the collapse of Germany in World War I persuaded Sikorsky to emmigrate to the United States. It was tough at first; he could not follow his dreams of inventing but had to become a lecturer and schoolteacher. Finally, with some other Russian officers, he formed the Sikorsky Aero Engineering Corporation. The company was located in an old barn near Roosevelt Field on Long Island, New York. Eventually, this outfit became a division of the United Aircraft Corporation, with a plant at Bridgeport, Connecticut, where the big Clipper flying boats were designed and produced. Igor Sikorsky became a United States citizen in 1928.

He could foresee that the flying boats would be replaced by other planes and decided to return to his helicopter project. This time, he had a trained engineering group he could command. He began his construction in 1939, and by September 14 of that year, he had the satisfaction of sitting at the controls and taking the first helicopter up. He thought that the helicopter would be used in industry and for rescue purposes, not foreseeing the many military uses for it. He maintained that the only predictions that he regretted were those that were too conservative.

Sikorsky retired in 1957 but remained as a consultant until his death in 1972. He received many honors and awards in the United States and Europe, including the United States Presidential Certificate of Merit in 1948.

Igor Sikorsky flies his VS-300 helicopter in 1939. The flight only lasted ten seconds. Sikorsky continued to experiment with the design over the next few years.

Planes in World War II

A poster exhorts maximum aircraft production during World War II. As men left for fighting duties, women moved in to work on airplane assembly lines and helped produce the more than 360,000 aircraft built during World War II.

As dictator Adolf Hitler's Germany began to threaten peace in Europe, other countries took another look at the potential power of military aircraft. Memories of World War I fanned fears of destruction with an air war. In fact, although they moved them around so Allied spies would think they had a much larger air force, the Germans had only about two hundred old planes at the beginning of World War II, compared to the twelve hundred planes a year and thousands of pilots America was producing by the end of World War I.

German bombers, like those of their enemies, weren't able to hit specific targets until near the end of the war. However, fear of what the Germans might do forced the countries that became the Allies in World War II (Britain, France, the U.S., China, and the Soviet Union) to draft new plans for military planes that had to be easy to mass-produce, repair, and maintain under combat conditions.

At first, although only supported by a small air force, the German troops easily defeated the poorly armed countries of Europe and appeared to be winning the war. The British had to withdraw to their island home, where they faced attack by rockets and airborne bombs. The air defense by the Royal Air Force in the Battle of Britain in 1940 against German planes was heroic.

POUR IT ON!

Then, Japan attacked the United States at Pearl Harbor, Hawaii, on December 7, 1941, with planes from its aircraft carriers. The Japanese had a small but efficient air force designed to support their army and navy. Because of this surprise attack, the United States was forced to enter the war.

The U.S. had begun to increase its production of military aircraft back when the war started in Europe. With this and the European effort, the Allies began to have air superiority over Europe by 1944. In Britain, Frank Whittle had developed the turbojet engine in 1941 for the Allies, and by the end of the war, these engines were powering the British Meteor fighters.

For most of World War II, strategic bombing remained inaccurate, but the air support of army and navy units was essential. Toward the end, the Germans developed the Messerschmitt Me 262, a jet fighter, and the pilotless rocket-propelled V-2, the first long-range ballistic missile. The Allies scrambled to find out about the rockets Germany was building. They were able to get an amazing amount of information and even some of the rockets through intelligence operations.

When they started the war in 1939, the Germans had believed it would be a short one and were satisfied with their production of seven hundred planes a month. However, toward the end of the war in 1944, they tried to produce four thousand planes a month and found that even this was not enough. The military on both sides of this war demanded a tremendous increase in both the numbers and the abilities of airplanes, promoting research and development far beyond what private industry would have done.

This progress came to a horrible climax in 1945, when the American Boeing B-29 Superfortress dropped atom bombs on Hiroshima and Nagasaki, causing the death and radioactive destruction that ended the war with Japan. World War II had radically changed the nature of warfare, demonstrated the importance of effective air power, and brought humanity into the nuclear age, ready or not, on the wings of its flying machines.

AMAZING FACTS

The very first jet turbine plane was the German Heinkel 178, which made its first successful flight in August 1939. Fortunately for the Allies, the Nazi air force (Luftwaffe) high command didn't see the jet's potential and ordered the inventor to put his energies into designing regular planes instead.

Frank Whittle

In deepest secrecy, the runway was cleared in a military airport. The engine revved into action. Lumbering down the runway, the first successful jet airplane shot into the air on May 15, 1941.

With the help of British engineer Frank Whittle, jet engines allowed airplanes to fly at high speed at high altitudes. Jet engines were simpler, with fewer moving parts than piston engines and more durable. By the end of World War II, jet planes had been tested and were in production. Whittle's engines were used in the British Gloster Meteor plane — the only jet used by the Allies in World War II.

Frank Whittle was born in Coventry, England, in 1907. His father was a mechanic with a small shop. Before Frank was a teenager, he learned how to use drills and lathes. His hobby was reading about aircraft engineering.

In 1923, he joined the Royal Air Force (RAF). After making an outstanding record in three years of learning aircraft assembly, he was sent to the RAF college for flight training. Following this, he received an assignment to a fighter squadron.

Whittle, with other people, recognized that what was needed in military aircraft was some kind of an engine that would let planes fly at high altitudes with

Frank Whittle explains his jet engine to the press in 1948.

high speed. He thought of the idea of using the jet power of a turbine engine instead of pistons. The officials of the Air Ministry, to whom he presented his idea, considered the notion impractical because of the stresses on the plane and of the high temperatures of a gas turbine engine.

However, Whittle did not give up on his idea and filed a patent on a turbojet engine in 1930. He continued to work on the project but could not interest others in the idea during the Depression years when money was tight. Five years later, when his patent came up for renewal, he was married with a family and did not come up with enough money to keep the patent in force.

A short time after that, with more money available, Whittle filed new patents and interested others in his idea. In 1936, he founded a company called Power Jets Limited. Tests of his newest engine revealed a number of problems, but money was not available even to replace parts of the machine damaged during test runs. It was not until the start of World War II in 1939 that he won a substantial backing of government funds.

The Gloster Meteor, a jet fighter, was used by the Allies in World War II from 1944.

The 1941 test of the engine in an airplane built by the Gloster Aircraft Company was just the first step. This E.28 craft flew at 370 miles per hour (596 kilometers per hour), beating the top speed of the Spitfire, then Britain's best fighter plane. By 1944, the new engine was to power Britain's Meteor plane.

Whittle retired from the RAF with the rank of air commodore and was knighted the same year. He was made a commander in the U.S. Legion of Merit in 1946 and, in 1977, he became a research professor at the U.S. Naval Academy.

— Chapter 3 —
Jets, Rockets, and Supersonic Transport

World War II radically changed aviation as engineers developed powerful jet engines and rockets, new navigation systems, and improvements in radar that made air travel safer. The war effort trained many pilots and built support systems such as airports and weather stations. Now, countries wanted to take these advances and apply them to peacetime uses.

Experimental and Research Planes

To make planes go even faster, the body, wings, and tail had to be redesigned. A Lockheed engineer, Clarence "Kelly" Johnson, had forecast in 1937 that there could be problems at two-thirds the speed of sound, or about 465 miles per hour (749 kilometers per hour). Pilots diving at that rate found the P-38 Lightning fighter planes and British Supermarine Spitfires both ran into problems, sometimes shaking out of control. Trying to discover if flight above this barrier was possible, many brave pilots risked death during the war to test new models of planes.

The British continued to make a determined effort to break the sound barrier. Geoffrey de Havilland, a famous aircraft designer, led the way. Unfortunately, his Swallow plane — piloted in 1946 by his son at speeds that may have exceeded 90 percent of the speed of sound — simply disintegrated, killing his son. De Havilland then tried the unpiloted, remote-controlled Vickys, but these, too, were lost.

Meanwhile, the United States had moved into the speed race. Bell Aircraft Corporation built the plane, known as the X-1, that Chuck Yeager flew in 1947 to break the sound barrier. With that barrier down, what lay ahead in supersonic speed?

Supersonic Advances

German rocket scientists had studied designs of rocket-powered aircraft that could fly beyond Mach 4 (four times the speed of sound). Now, the United States investigated supersonic flight.

The Bell X-1 and X-2 and the Douglas D-588-2 Skyrocket had pushed plane speeds just beyond Mach 2. However, at this time, wind tunnels could not provide the conditions in which to test aircraft that went beyond Mach 4. Pilots would have to test them in real supersonic flights. The skin of the airplane would have to be able to take high temperatures, and the plane would have to be stable enough to go through the sound barrier and atmosphere and then land. In 1954, plans were developed for such a plane, and in 1955, pilots took the X-15 to nearly Mach 7 and more than 67 miles (107 kilometers) above Earth — a world altitude record for a winged aircraft.

> ### AMAZING FACTS
>
> X-15 jets are launched into flight from beneath the starboard wing of a flying B-52 Stratofortress bomber. Although X-15s still hold the record for the fastest powered flight of a winged aircraft, shuttle orbiters reenter Earth's atmosphere from space faster, at speeds of over Mach 20.

The X-15 hypersonic aircraft was flown at an altitude of over sixty miles (ninety-seven kilometers). Because space is considered to begin at fifty miles (eighty kilometers) above Earth's surface, X-15 pilots who went this high were awarded astronauts' wings.

The Space Program and Nonstop Global Travel

Information from the X-15 was turned over to the space program, which shortened the time needed to build the space shuttle — a reusable spacecraft.

By 1969, plans for the shuttle began to take shape, and the contract was awarded to Rockwell International in 1972. But it was not until 1981 that the shuttle completed its first mission, reaching a speed of Mach 25 and an orbit around the earth 150 miles (240 kilometers) high. Since then, the shuttle has made many trips, increasing our knowledge of Earth and space.

Not all experiments are about speed. Burt Rutan designed a strange looking plane that would be the first to fly around the world without refueling. It was built with money from sponsors and used volunteer help to build, test, and plan the route. The plane, named the *Voyager*, was flown by Dick Rutan and Jeanna Yeager. They crammed themselves into a tiny cockpit so that most of the rest of the plane — including its strange wing formation — carried the fuel: 489 gallons (1,853 liters) of oil, or three-fourths of the craft's take-off weight. In 1986, after nine days, three minutes, and forty-four seconds in the air, they had their world record.

The twin-engine propeller plane Voyager, *designed by Burt Rutan, flew nonstop around the world — more than twenty-four thousand miles (thirty-eight thousand kilometers) — in nine days in 1986. This was possible because* Voyager *was made of ultralight materials and consisted mainly of fuel tanks.*

Jet Engines and Military Planes

After World War II, a great surplus of planes existed and money for military uses was being cut. However, the cold war, with its competition between the East (the former Soviet Union, its satellites, and allies) and the West (primarily the United States, Great Britain, and Western European nations) provided a new incentive for producing new and up-to-date models.

Introduced in 1947, the Boeing B-47 Stratojet bomber was an important weapon. It had a thirty-five degree swept-back wing design and six jet engines — a design that was to influence future planes. The plane had an impressive bombing system and could travel at speeds that made interception by fighter planes difficult. It was called a "defensive weapon" because its threat helped deter the use of nuclear weapons by the other side.

A Boeing B-47 Stratojet bomber edges toward the boom of a refueling tanker. After World War II, bomber ranges were extended by the use of in-flight refueling.

The Soviet Union developed the MiG-15 jet fighter, considered the equal of the fine fighters produced by the Western countries. In the 1950s, the American F-86 Sabre challenged this MiG-15 in combat when the Soviet Union supplied planes and pilots to the North Koreans during the Korean War.

After World War II, helicopters became safer and more efficient. The military successfully made use of helicopters during wars in Korea, Vietnam, and the Persian Gulf. This helicopter is ferrying troops in Vietnam.

Because the commercial sector did not immediately turn to jet engines for their planes, it was difficult for civilians to get access to jets in order to set speed records. U.S. Air Force Reserve officer Jacqueline Cochran asked the military for the chance to fly a jet plane but was turned down. She had to become a consultant to the Canadian government to train in a jet. The daughter of the French president, Jacqueline Auriol, had an easier time in gaining access to jets. Both women set speed records.

Advances in the 1950s and 1960s focused less on the structural designs of planes and more on parts engineering. Great improvements were made in navigation, radar, safety, and fire control. For the first time, computers played a role not only in the design of aircraft but also as an aid to the pilot. New weapons and control systems were developed. Unfortunately, with all these advances, the cost of planes also increased.

Commercial Aviation

Meanwhile in the commercial sector, World War II also had its effect on civilian postwar travel. People could now travel long distances in shorter periods of time. Surplus planes were available, and more luxurious models were introduced.

In 1947, Pan American Airlines offered world travel in "Connie," Lockheed's L-749 Constellation, which Trans World Airlines (TWA) and American Overseas Airline also used. Boeing's 377 Stratocruiser, a double-decker passenger plane, and the Douglas C-54 (with various model changes and DC numbers) also provided luxury travel. These planes were modern but did not use jet engines, relying instead on piston engines with propellers.

The first commercial use of all-jet engines was introduced by the British company de Havilland in 1952. Its Comet 1A carried thirty-six passengers at a cruising speed of 500 miles per hour (805 kilometers per hour). However, two years later, two of the Comets broke up in flight. Engineers discovered that the metal could not take the repeated pressurization from flights. The Comet was redesigned but did not recapture public confidence.

An American company, Boeing, produced a highly successful jet airliner in 1954 — the Boeing 707. Since the start-up costs for this plane were more than $16 million, Boeing was gambling that it could make a profit. By 1967, 568 of these planes were in service, even though they were more expensive to operate than older designs. The engineers wanted to approach the speed of sound yet still maintain low fuel consumption. Few of the subsonic planes of today travel any faster than the speeds set by the 707.

By the 1960s, the airlines wanted larger planes that could carry more passengers efficiently. The Boeing 727 and 747 "Jumbo Jet," the Douglas DC-10, and Lockheed's L1011 all met these needs. Now, planes could carry as many as five hundred passengers. New materials were developed to reduce the weight of planes and therefore save fuel costs.

Jacqueline Cochran (1906?–1980)

Jackie Cochran did the seemingly impossible. At a time when jet test pilots were exclusively male, she not only flew jets (rare enough) but also set records in them.

Cochran grew up in poverty. Orphaned when she was four years old, she did not know who her parents were or how she had come to the foster family with whom she lived. She also did not know when she was born, though she gave dates that ranged from 1906 to 1910. She wore dresses made of flour sacks and had no shoes until she was eight years old.

From Florida, her foster family moved to Georgia, where she worked in a cotton mill, pushing a cart between looms. She earned $4.50 a week and worked twelve hours a day. Then, at age ten, she went to work in a beauty shop doing odd jobs. She chose her last name from a phone book when she was a teenager. In those days and under those working conditions, it's not too surprising that Cochran had only a year of formal education. One teacher taught her to read, and she read her way to the education she had.

In 1932, she inquired about flight training. Cochran soloed after her third day of flight instruction and took her examination and received her license in three weeks. She quit her job as a beauty operator and devoted more time to obtaining advanced flying instruction.

Cochran established her own cosmetic business, which provided her with the time and money to pursue her interest in flying. In 1937, she achieved a women's national speed record of 292.27 miles (470.55 kilometers) per hour. In the 1938 Bendix race, she was first in a field of nine men. From 1937 through 1950, she was awarded the Harmon Trophy for the year's finest aviation achievement by a female pilot.

By the time World War II broke out, only three other women held more international records than Cochran. During the war, Cochran was director of flight training of the Women's Air Force Service Pilots (WASPS). This organization trained women fliers to ferry aircraft where needed and to simulate combat situations. More than one thousand women were trained as WASPS, and Cochran was awarded the Distinguished Service Medal for her work.

After the war, in a surplus U.S. fighter plane that she had modified, she set a new speed record. However, if she was to continue to set new speed records, she needed a jet plane rather than one with a piston engine. Even though she held a commission as a lieutenant colonel, the U.S. military refused to give her permission to fly one.

Jackie Cochran was director of the Women's Air Force Service Pilots (WASPS) during World War II. Here, a group of WASPS, with parachutes slung over their back, head to their planes.

A friend suggested that she try for a chance to fly a Canadian jet. She landed a job as a consultant to Canadair to try speed tests with the Sabre plane before it was turned over to the Canadian Air Force. She calculated that she spent over one hundred hours in ground study for every hour of flying time in the Sabre. She flew at official speeds of over Mach 1 (the sound barrier) in 1953. Later, she went on to set many more speed records.

Cochran's flying came to an end when she began having fainting spells in 1970 and had a pacemaker implanted to normalize her heart beat. She died on August 9, 1980. At her funeral, Chuck Yeager declared, "Sometimes even Jackie Cochran couldn't believe what she had accomplished."

The introduction of large planes like the Boeing 747 shown here required innovations in support systems — airports that could handle larger groups of passengers, longer runways, and maintenance operations to handle more parts.

The 1960s also saw the first efforts to use supersonic flight for commercial planes. The British and French Concorde was designed to travel at Mach 2 speed, high up in the stratosphere. The United States backed away from funding further research on the Supersonic Transports (SSTs) because of their high cost.

Smaller Planes

As early as 1957, Lockheed introduced the first all-jet small plane. Two years later Grumman produced the Gulfstream, with its twin turboprop engine. A very popular entry to this field in 1964 was the Learjet, with six seats and a top speed of 500 miles per hour (805 kilometers per hour).

Several crashes of small commercial planes brought about changes in safety rules. Commuter planes originally had to meet fewer safety regulations than the big planes. However, commuter pilots must make many more takeoffs and landings from airports not equipped with the latest technology.

Since World War II, aviation has undergone great developments in flying techniques. Inventions in many industries have helped bring about these advances and will continue to do so as new ways are found to transport people and cargo in the sky.

— Chapter 4 —
How Planes Work

At the beginning of aviation, people often asked how something heavier than air could stay up in the sky. Even today, when people get on an airplane, some stop to wonder how the thing can ever get off the ground without at least flapping its wings! However, once a large commercial airliner is gliding smoothly through the air, it often feels more like a crowded living room with food service than a flying machine — at least when it flies in good weather.

Even for seasoned airplane travelers, the principles of air flight are usually a mystery, although the reason airplanes can fly is fairly simple. There are four forces that govern the flight of an airplane: gravity, lift, drag, and thrust.

Forces for Flight

Gravity is the force that pulls all objects toward the ground and keeps them (and us) from floating off into space. Lift is created by the movement of the plane's wing through the air and works because the pressure of air decreases as its speed, or velocity, increases. Airplane wings are designed so that airflow moves faster (with less pressure) over the curved top of the wing than it does along the wing's flat underside. So the faster a plane moves through the air, the more lift occurs from the greater pressure pushing up the underside of the wing.

Lift also occurs because wings are designed to move through the air at an angle that deflects, or pushes, air downward, which in turn pushes the airplane upward. This is in accordance with

> **AMAZING FACTS**
>
> The Coanda Effect is a quirk of nature you can observe if you pour water from a pitcher of just the right shape. The water will curl back around the underside of the spout and slide down the side of the pitcher. Both water and air tend to follow the slope of a properly curved surface, so airplane designs for some aircraft use the Coanda Effect to improve a wing's lift. The wings are designed so that the exhaust of jet engines follows the curve of the wing's trailing edge flaps, blowing to the rear and down to help the airplane move up and forward.

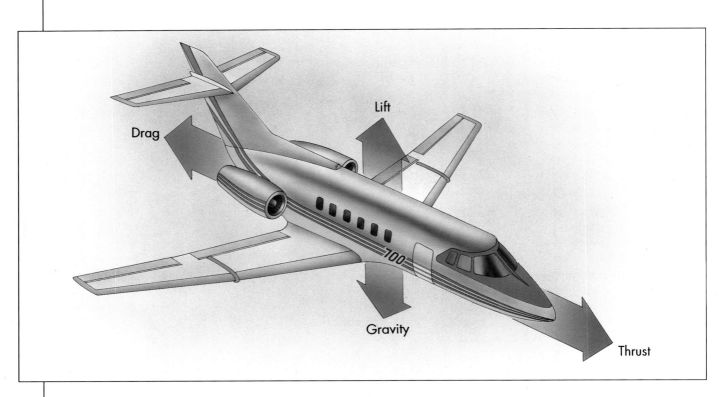

Four forces work on an airplane. Lift, created by the shape of the wings, exerts a force to oppose gravity while thrust, from the engine, has to oppose drag.

Sir Isaac Newton's third law of physics, the study of how energy and matter interact. Newton's third law explains that every action must have an equal and opposite reaction. For airplanes, this also means that the exhaust gases from the back of the jet or rocket engine or the airstream leaving the propeller push the plane in the opposite direction, causing it to move forward. This forward force is called thrust. Drag is the force of air opposing, or pushing against, an airplane's forward movement. When flying at constant speed, thrust equals drag.

Other Forces at Work on a Plane

Weight exerts a downward force in response to gravity and must be taken into account when flying an airplane. The weight of the aircraft itself (and whatever it carries, including fuel, cargo, and passengers) must be measured in relation to lift, drag, and thrust. As fuel is used up in flight, this causes a decrease in the weight, which allows the plane to fly with less effort.

It is lift and thrust overcoming gravity and drag that get the plane up in the air. Of course, in an airplane that takes off straight up, lift and thrust are both upward, as they are in helicopters and in the vertical/short takeoff and landing aircraft, known as V/STOLs.

The force of air, or atmosphere, creates both lift and drag. However, our atmosphere is not as simple as we would think. Dust, moisture, water vapor, wind, and turbulence affect it. Variations in air pressure, temperature, and density change the speed of sound through air, so when a plane flies faster than the speed of sound, we have to remember that the speed of sound, and thus the speed of the plane, is faster or slower depending on the atmospheric conditions of the time.

The speed and pressure of a flying airplane disrupt the smooth flow of air around the plane. If the plane is flying at slower speeds, the air has more time to adjust. When the plane moves at higher speeds, a pressure shock wave is built up in front of the plane. This wave affects the lifting power of the air and creates control and stability problems for the pilot. This phenomenon is known as compressibility.

Faster than the Competition

Since one of the great values of an airplane is its speed, it's not surprising that there has been a push toward building faster planes. High-speed flight begins at 350 miles per hour (564 kilometers per hour), less than half the speed of sound. High speed is measured by Mach (pronounced MOCK) numbers. Below 350 miles per hour, the air does not compress and create the problems it causes flight at higher speeds. As speed comes close to Mach 1 (the speed of sound), the buffeting caused by this compressibility affects the flight. As speed approaches Mach 2, the temperature surrounding the plane gets so hot that aluminum loses it strength. New designs and materials have to be used. The faster a plane goes, the more problems have to be solved.

AMAZING FACTS

Some aircraft are designed to take off and land with their wings straight out but can move their wings into a swept-back position for high speed flight, as many birds do. The General Dynamics F-111, Grumman F-14, and Panavia Tornado are all examples of swing-wing aircraft.

Geoffrey de Havilland in his two-seater airplane, the Moth, in 1928.

Geoffrey de Havilland, Sr. (1882–1965)

The Englishman Sir Geoffrey de Havilland's long career spanned the years from the Wright brothers' discovery to the jet age and supersonic flight. Early on, he demonstrated his engineering ability when, at boarding school, he built his own motorbike.

De Havilland began his career as a designer of buses until he heard of the reports of the Wright brothers' flights. Then he asked his grandfather to lend him money so that he could quit his job and build an airplane engine. The first plane that he designed and manufactured with his friend, Frank Hearle, was made out of wire, wood, and linen. His wife sewed the fabric that was to make the wings. In 1909, he finished the plane that took off, went forty yards (thirty-six meters), and then crashed. He built another one with greater success. However, his grandfather's loan was used up, and he had to go back to work.

De Havilland continued to work on new designs. In 1916, he introduced a plane made of wood, with no windshield and no brakes. However, the plane was sturdy and could fly and maneuver at nearly 100 miles per hour (160 kilometers per hour). The British used it in the early phases of World War I until de Havilland came up with two improved models.

After World War I, he formed his own aircraft company and produced a two-seater plane called the Moth. It was inexpensive, easy to operate, and was one of the most successful light airplanes in the history of aviation. It was credited with starting the flying club movement and training large numbers of amateur pilots who met the needs of the expanded Royal Air Force during World War II.

During World War II, de Havilland and his company built twenty-three thousand airplanes for the Allies. Best known was the Mosquito, a fast, light bomber made of plywood because of the scarcity of steel. Because of its speed, it could outrun fighters, and in sixty days alone, it shot down six hundred of the long-range V-1 flying bombs that the Germans sent against Britain. His younger son, John, was killed while test flying this plane.

The de Havilland Mosquito light bomber was one of the most successful airplanes of World War II.

Geoffrey de Havilland went on to produce jet fighters, the Vampire and the Venom, that could travel 500 miles per hour (805 kilometers per hour). He pioneered a commercial jet plane, the Comet, and D.H. "Ghost" jet engines. In 1946, he built the D.H. 108, called the Swallow, with no tail and wings that swept back at a forty-degree angle. These design features were introduced to cut down on the buffeting effect of the air friction at high speeds. His other son, Geoffrey de Havilland, Jr., tried for the world record speed of 616 miles per hour (992 kilometers per hour). It is guessed that he achieved at least Mach .90. However, the plane disintegrated in the sky, and the pilot was killed.

De Havilland was knighted in 1944 and was awarded the Order of Merit in 1962.

Terms for flight speed all include the term sonic, which means of or related to audible sound. Below Mach 1, speed is subsonic; above, supersonic. Speeds right at Mach 1 are called transonic. Above Mach 5, speed is called hypersonic.

Parts of a Plane

The body of the plane is called the *fuselage* and houses the pilot, passengers, cargo, controls, and sometimes the engine. The shape of the fuselage is streamlined as much as possible to cut down on the drag force, the force that exerts the backward push.

Lift is provided by wing shape. Looking at the wing from the side of the plane gives an *airfoil* section, while looking down on the shape of the wing gives the *planform* shape. These two shapes, together with the placement of the wing on the fuselage, will vary depending on what task the plane must do. The pilot steers the plane by controlling *yaw* (turning the plane to the left or right), *pitch* (pointing the airplane up or down), and *roll* (rolling the wing from side to side).

The engine that produces the thrust force is called a *powerplant*. Five basic kinds of engines power most aircraft: the piston, turbojet, turboprop, turbofan, and propfan engines. The first is a piston engine similar to an automobile's engine except it turns a plane's propeller (or prop) instead of a car's drive shaft. Piston engines drove all aircraft until 1939, when the jet engine was successfully used on a full-sized aircraft. The turbojet, or jet for short, is an engine that takes air in through the front, compresses it, and mixes it with fuel. When this mixture is ignited in the combustion chamber, the hot gases thrust out the rear of the engine and push the aircraft forward. A turbojet is faster than the piston-engined prop plane but uses much more fuel.

The other three engines use the turbine core of the jet engine in different ways. The turboprop uses it to power a propeller. This gives the aircraft about the same maximum speed as a propeller driven by the piston engine and is typically used for short-

---

AMAZING FACTS

Planned for the 1990s and beyond for both commercial and military planes in the United States, France, Britain, Germany and China, propfan planes may bring propellers back to aircraft of all sizes by the year 2000.

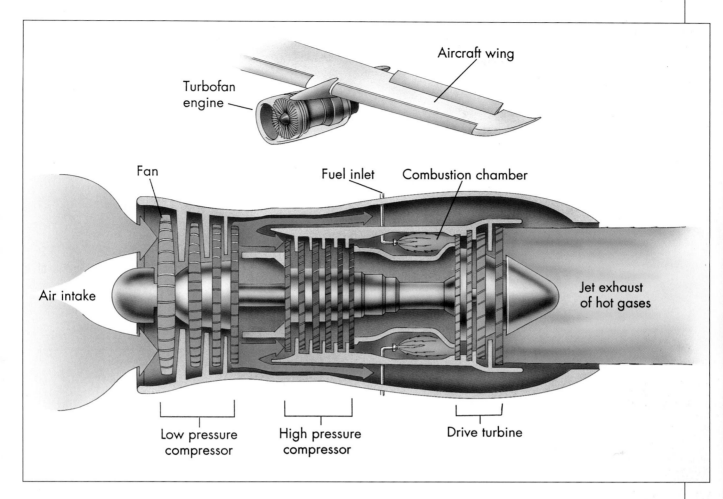

Turbofan engine

Aircraft wing

Fan

Fuel inlet

Combustion chamber

Air intake

Jet exhaust of hot gases

Low pressure compressor

High pressure compressor

Drive turbine

range flights. The turbofan adds a fan in front of the jet engine to provide about three times more thrust than the turbojet. The propfan engine turns propeller blades that are curved to spin faster than straight propellers. It provides speeds typical of present-day commercial jetliners with only three-fourths of the fuel needed by turbofans.

Piston and jet engines each have four stages: intake, compression, combustion, and exhaust. However, in the jet fuel burns continuously, while in the piston engine, combustion takes place only once in the revolution of the engine.

Planes that have propellers use air differently than jets do. Propellers on the piston-type engine move large quantities of air slowly, while jets move small quantities of air extremely fast.

The turbofan is the most commonly used jet engine. The fan sends air to the engine to be mixed with the fuel for combustion and also around the engine for additional thrust. The hot gases produced by the combustion spin a turbine that drives the low and high pressure compressors. The escaping gases provide thrust for the airplane.

This computerized aircraft instrument panel shows runway approach information at the top. The radar weather map below marks the positions of two navigation beacons (pink and green). Above them, the white arc is a compass on which the aircraft is marked as a white triangle.

The Computer as Copilot

As planes and their tasks become more complex, there is greater need for instruments such as the altimeters, which tell the pilot how high the plane is, and airspeed indicators, which show how fast the plane is going. The pilot also needs to keep track of other planes through radar.

The faster the pilot must make decisions and the more instruments there are on board, the more a computer is needed. The computer can rapidly process the information fed to it from instruments and free the pilot to control the craft.

Support Services are Essential

Planes wouldn't work very well without the ground support services they receive. Airports provide not only runways but refueling, deicing, repairs, and changes in crews, passengers, and cargo. With so much air traffic now using the skies, control towers and rules and regulations concerning flight are necessary. Air travel has become increasingly popular, so ticketing and food supplies for airplanes have become more complex and usually need computer assistance to keep things moving quickly and correctly.

The increase in flights has also brought increased risks. Governments must supply extra immigration, health, and custom officers at airports to keep up with the passenger flow and check for potential hazards that might be smuggled into the country.

With a complex invention like the airplane, inventions and discoveries from many different fields have been incorporated to improve the performance of the craft. These advances in technology affect not only the design of the plane but also the support services needed for its successful operation.

Finally, teamwork is the invisible but essential force that maintains the airplane industry. We've looked at the aerodynamic reasons, the engines and mechanical supports, and the atmospheric conditions that allow aircraft to fly, but no plane today can leave the runway without teams of people who work with other teams to get us in the air. From the cooperative groups who design and manufacture the aircraft to the ground crew on which the pilots and in-flight crew depend, cooperative effort is the way all aircraft, even one-seaters for solo pilots, are able to soar. In addition, air traffic controllers are the pilot's partner on the ground, while ticket agents provide the link between the passengers' travel plans and the airlines' travel routes. It's no wonder that the first successful flight came from the first team in aviation, the Wright brothers. In terms of teamwork, we've been following their example ever since.

Inside the air traffic control tower at San Francisco International Airport. The green radar displays show aircraft flying within fifty-five miles (ninety kilometers) of the airport.

— Chapter 5 —
Military Planes Today

Military planes account for some of the most unusual aircraft designs found today. The military needs planes with speed, maneuverability, and the ability to fly at high altitudes. When planning for military operations, leaders can't know when they may be called into combat, who the enemy will be, or where the enemy will be located, but they must provide the planes and missiles to meet the challenges that face their nations. Readiness is the key to victory.

Military planes perform many functions, from fighting to spying, and must operate against different kinds of enemies and over all kinds of land and water. Air forces need the ability to move their equipment and that of fighting forces over long distances in a short period of time. They must be able to deal with defensive maneuvers of the enemy, including enemy troops or missile launchers that move around to try to escape detection.

Radar Sounds the Alarm

Radar warns of approaching enemy aircraft, so that missiles can be directed to lock onto the plane and destroy it. It was developed between 1935 and 1940 independently in several different countries and can not only detect where an object is but also sense how fast it is moving. It measures the distance to a target by sending out a radio signal and then recording the time needed for the echo that bounces off the target to return to the source. Two kinds of radar can be used: Acquisition radar will detect planes several hundred miles away, while tracking radar,

---

AMAZING FACTS

The Convair B-58 Hustler was the world's first supersonic bomber. It flew from New York to Paris, France, in a little over three hours in 1961.

A painting by W. T. Rawlinson of a radar station on the British coast during the Battle of Britain in 1940. The development of radar helped warn the Allies of German air raids. British Hurricane and Spitfire fighters could then attack the German planes that bombed Britain day and night.

with a fifty-mile (eighty-kilometer) range, more accurately directs gunfire or missiles against the target.

There are many defensive maneuvers against radar, including flying low to the ground where echoes are not so accurate or jamming it by sending out a more powerful radio wave. Some planes distract the radar by dropping chaff (small metal filaments) or firing electromagnetic pulses, while others deceive it by towing a target behind the plane that attracts the missile.

Sneaking Past Radar

The most secretive flyers are the stealth fighters and bombers. These are designed so that they have no surfaces that can be picked up by radar. One of the most surprising of these is the Lockheed F-117A Stealth fighter. With light-absorbing paint and windows coated to reduce any reflected light, it is intended for use at night. Its jet engines have been constructed to reduce noise and are positioned above the wing with a cooling system to

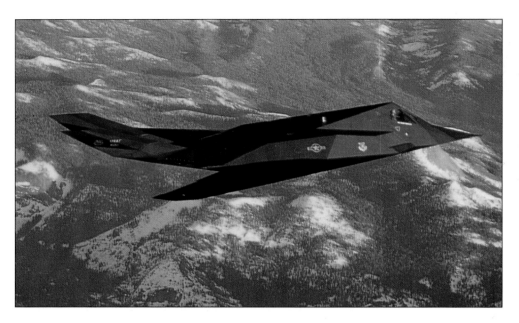

Although the Lockheed F-117A Stealth fighter has a forty-three-foot (thirteen-meter) wingspan and a sixty-six-foot (twenty-meter) length, it reflects about the same amount of radar energy as a hummingbird. During the Persian Gulf War, it dropped bombs on Iraqi targets with pinpoint precision.

reduce the heat that ground-based heat-seeking missiles might target. Moreover, the many angles of the plane deflect radar signals to the side and back, so it can fly quite secretly through enemy airspace. Another secret flyer, the Northrup B-2 stealth bomber, has a saw-tooth wing shape.

Lessons from the Persian Gulf War

When Iraq invaded Kuwait and threatened Saudi Arabia in 1990, the Western world and other Arab nations rallied to the support of the threatened Arab countries. The Persian Gulf War was a proving ground for recently developed aviation technology.

The Gulf War was unique because it relied on technology so much that few lives were lost on the U.S. side, and it introduced the world to the remarkable stealth planes in battle. This war also showed the effectiveness of missiles that could be guided to their targets without human pilots, which cut down on the need for pilot-flown missions and therefore the risk of combat death.

In this war, eight McDonnell Douglas AH-64 Apache helicopters, guided by a U.S. Air Force special operations Sikorsky CH-53, flew in at the start to knock out two of the key enemy radar sites guarding the corridor to Baghdad, the capital of Iraq. The Apaches attacked tanks, artillery, and infantry bunkers to support ground operations.

Interceptors, Interdictors, and Spy Planes

As early as World War I, the military recognized the need to be able to intercept spy or fighter planes and shoot them down. In the Persian Gulf War, most of the thirty-nine Iraqi aircraft destroyed in combat were knocked out by the McDonnell Douglas F-15C Eagle using the Raytheon/General Dynamics AIM-7 Sparrow missile.

Now, four European nations are cooperating to design and build a new interceptor to be delivered in the late 1990s to the air forces of Britain, Germany, Italy, and Spain. This plane will turn rapidly and have enough power to gain speed or altitude quickly after a combat maneuver.

Cutting off an enemy's communication and supply lines is the function of an interdictor. These planes have to be able to counter a great variety of defensive systems of the enemy.

The F-4G, called the "Wild Weasel," could operate alone in Desert Storm but more often were part of a larger strike force. They could force through defenses, providing a corridor for other planes to use safely.

While a great deal of intelligence information can be gathered from satellite photos, there is still a need for planes to transmit data about strategic and tactical changes. The two main systems that did this in the Persian Gulf operation were the Boeing F-3 Sentry Airborne Warning and Control System (AWACS) and the Lockheed TR-1A, a battlefield observation aircraft. Also rushed to battle before all testing had been completed were the Boeing E-8 JSTARS (Joint Surveillance Target Attack Radar System), aircraft that can detect the buildup of forces far behind enemy lines and then send information to ground and air forces waiting to strike these targets.

AMAZING FACTS

The Lockheed C-5 Galaxy is the world's largest aircraft. The C-5 can carry 265,000 pounds (119,000 kilograms) of people, supplies, and vehicles for up to 2,500 miles (4,000 kilometers). Aiding the U.S. withdrawal from Vietnam, the C-5 carried a single load of twenty-two light helicopters. It is wide enough to hold an eight-lane bowling alley and is longer than the Wright brothers' first flight.

Guion "Guy" S. Bluford, Jr.

Colonel Guy Bluford was the first African-American in space and has made three other space flights. But his imagination may have taken flight from model airplanes.

Bluford was born in 1942 in Philadelphia, the oldest of three sons. His father, an inventor and mechanical engineer, and his mother, a public school teacher, had high expectations for their sons. Guy was a quiet loner who liked crossword puzzles and games with a mental challenge. But his construction of model airplanes probably sparked his interest in how planes flew. By high school, he had decided to become an aerospace engineer.

However, his high school guidance counselor was not so sure that Bluford was college material. The boy seemed to have to work harder at school. Nevertheless, Bluford went to Pennsylvania State University and earned his B.S. degree in aerospace engineering in 1964.

He won his wings that year, trained in the F-4C Phantom, and was sent off for combat in Vietnam in 1967. He flew 144 combat missions in the war, dropping bombs and napalm in support of ground forces. Of Guy Bluford's 144 combat missions, some 60 were over the Hanoi area where he saw plenty of antiaircraft

Guy Bluford, right, and NASA colleagues during a zero-gravity training flight.

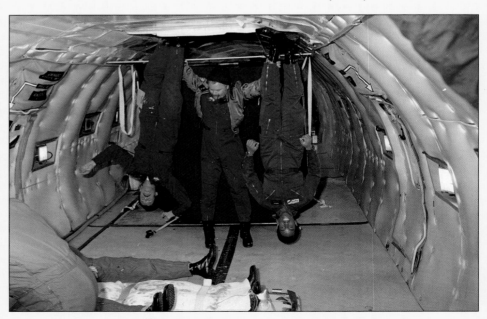

artillery. When he could save some of the ground forces with his missions, he found it "most gratifying."

After serving in Vietnam, Bluford studied in the Air Force Institute of Technology at the Wright-Patterson base in Dayton, Ohio. In 1973, he earned his M.S. degree in aerospace engineering with distinction and, in 1977, was completing a doctorate in aerospace engineering with a minor in laser physics.

While he was very happy in his job as chief of the air dynamics and airframe branch of the Flight Dynamics Laboratory at the Wright-Patterson base, Bluford knew that he had to consider keeping up his flight skills. He started looking for a job at the same time that NASA began looking for pilot astronauts and mission-specialist astronauts. At the last minute, Bluford decided to put in his application and was selected as a mission-specialist astronaut, one of thirty-five chosen out of ten thousand individuals under consideration.

Guy Bluford tries out a treadmill on the space shuttle Challenger *during a 1983 mission.*

Training at NASA was tough, but Bluford testifies to the fun and enjoyment of his space experience. Bouncing around in gravity-free space and looking out at the superb views of Earth makes his work "exhilarating" according to his account. Bluford has added to our knowledge on his four space flights by his work with satellites, the robotic arm, and experiments in the space lab.

When asked what advice he would give to African-American young people, Bluford recommends: "Aim high! . . . Set goals. Be persistent. You can do anything you set your mind to. You've got to decide that you want to put in the hard work and perspiration to do it. Once you do that — you're on your way."

The Harrier is a vertical/short takeoff and landing (V/STOL) aircraft. It proved its worth in the 1982 Falklands War between Great Britain and Argentina and in use by the United States Marine Corps.

Strategic Fighters

To get in and out of tight places requires an aircraft that doesn't need a long runway. Two such planes are the British (V/STOL) Harrier and the United States Apache helicopter.

The Harrier is an impressive fixed-wing aircraft that can take off vertically like a helicopter and even hover in midair and make adjustments in position. In spite of its huge size, it moves with surprising precision. It is a bit frightening to see it perched overhead, hovering and making a tremendous noise as it moves like a huge mechanical hummingbird, up, over, or down a foot at a time.

Naval Air Power and Beyond

The navy shares many of the same needs for effective control of the air and seas that are found in land operations. It must be able to strike targets and defend itself. Navy aircraft carriers carry a variety of aircraft and support ships but can be an easy target of other ships or enemy air strikes.

More flexible because of its ability to work equally well on the surface or deep beneath the waves, a submarine can hide and then position itself to launch missiles at a target, thus combining the advantages of stealth and significant striking capabilities over a wide territory.

The military forces of a superpower such as the United States must be able to defend and attack anywhere in the world. This requires ongoing development of new planes and missiles and tactics for their use that are effective against whatever an enemy can devise.

AMAZING FACTS

To test the range of temperatures from air friction that a proposed fighter will have to face, aircraft engineers have, among other tests, painted heat-sensitive phosphorous onto a model of the plane before sending it into a high-pressure wind tunnel.

Chapter 6
Civilian Planes and the Future of Aviation

When supersonic flight was first introduced, people around the world were thrilled with the idea. Many nations hurried to design passenger planes that could take advantage of this new potential. However, in commercial aviation, the high speed and altitude so important for military planes do not necessarily help make high profits. The cost to the passenger or shipper must be taken into account. If fuel costs are more in a high-flying plane or if the faster aircraft is limited to fewer passengers, the price can be too high for the commercial plane market.

Partly because of these concerns, governments got involved in financing some of the first supersonic transports (SSTs). In 1968, two months before the British-French Concorde would fly, the Soviet Union produced the Tupolev-144, the first SST. Boeing had designed an SST model for the United States, but in 1971, the Senate refused to provide money to fund the project. Then, at the 1973 Paris air show, the Soviet plane was flown beyond its design capability and broke up in the air. In spite of this tragedy, the Soviet SST program was not terminated until 1984.

The Concorde

The British-French Concorde succeeded in finding customers able to pay the high price of supersonic transport. A supersonic flight is the closest thing to space travel that an ordinary citizen can get. The sky becomes dark blue. Clouds below travel toward the

> **AMAZING FACTS**
>
> The sonic boom comes from two shock waves that are made by the front and the tail of the plane. The shock waves from other parts of the plane tend to merge with these two main jolts, or booms, and sound like a double clap of thunder. Serious complaints about noise and broken windows have forced limitations on the flight paths over land at supersonic speed.

A Concorde rises after takeoff. In order to give the pilot a clear view, the nose of the plane is pointed down when it is on the ground and during takeoff. When flying supersonically, the nose is raised to cut down on air friction.

AMAZING FACTS

A team effort created the Concorde. After team-designing the craft, over eight hundred subcontractors and suppliers and some twenty-four thousand workers were required to put the huge jet into operation. The Concorde's wingspan is 83 feet, 10 inches (25.5 meters) and the plane is over 203 feet (61.9 meters) long and 40 feet (12.2 meters) high. It can reach a maximum supersonic speed of 1,370 miles per hour (2,206 kilometers per hour) over the ocean and a maximum subsonic speed of about 600 miles per hour (960 kilometers per hour) over land.

horizon in a circular pattern. Concorde accelerates rapidly: In just twenty seconds, the plane reaches 220 miles per hour (354 kilometers per hour). Flying at an altitude of 55,000 feet (16,750 meters), about 20,000 feet (6,700 meters) above the level of conventional airliners, it can land at 180 miles per hour (290 kilometers per hour), using carbon brakes to stop the plane quite suddenly.

However, this remarkable aircraft has a number of drawbacks. Tickets are expensive because of the high cost of the fuel it needs, and it has limited passenger seats — 100 compared to 375 on the larger competing aircraft, such as the Airbus. Because of complaints about sonic booms (the noise and pressure that occurs when a plane speeds through the sound barrier), the Concorde is sometimes forced to use routes over water. Sometimes this detour causes a longer flight than a short land route.

But overall, passenger satisfaction with the Concorde is very high. A flight across the Atlantic takes just three hours, compared to eight by conventional aircraft. Since Western Europe is five hours ahead of the United States' Eastern Standard Time, people flying from France, for example, could leave Paris at noon and arrive in New York at ten in the morning local time, two hours earlier than when they took off! For wealthy travelers, international business executives, and diplomats, this time saving is often worth the extra money. If bigger SSTs are built, perhaps the cost of travel can be cut and more people can take advantage of the speed of supersonic flight. On the other hand, the high cost of developing new planes may prove to be a barrier. The Concorde cost over $2 billion to develop.

Transport Planes Become Fuel Efficient

Using less fuel and carrying more passengers than supersonic transport, subsonic planes have been capturing most of the large airplane orders. Looking to the future, Boeing Company has invested more than $4 billion in designing its 777 that can carry 305 passengers in a three classes (first, business, and cabin) or 440 people in a single-class plane. The company will be in competition with the McDonnell Douglas three-engine MD-11 and the Airbus Industrie A330 and A340.

A Boeing 777 in production. Each of these twin-engine, wide body jets, designed for long overseas routes, will cost $100 million.

As jet planes became a status symbol for more corporations, new designs were developed. Burt Rutan, who designed the round-the-world nonstop *Voyager*, was asked by Beech Aircraft to come up with new ideas. The Beech Starship that resulted seems likely to shake up the industry. This plane has a new design, new materials, and new manufacturing techniques. The complete body of the plane can now be manufactured in twenty-eight hours instead of the nine days required of more usual planes.

Aircraft for Fun and Recreation

In the fifties, many predicted that airplanes would soon be as common as automobiles for Americans. High-quality planes such as Cessnas, Pipers, and the Beech Bonanza seemed to fit the bill. However, air flight is more weather dependent than the automobile and is better suited to long-distance travel than a trip to the supermarket. In addition, a small plane remains much more expensive than a car, and fuel costs are greater as well.

Nonetheless, people are generally in love with airplanes. Some people enjoy the hobby of collecting and preserving antique planes. Museums such as the National Air and Space Museum of the Smithsonian Institution help us appreciate the remarkable developments in flying in the twentieth century.

Many brave enthusiasts enjoy gliding, ballooning, parachuting, hang-gliding, and air-surfing. Each of these sports requires some knowledge of how aircraft work. Some gain their first aeronautic knowledge with model planes, which require skill both in construction and flying. What child (or office worker, for that matter) hasn't studied the art of making paper airplanes?

The Red Arrows flying team entertains at an air show. These shows displaying exciting and unusual planes, including ones that use human or solar power, attract thousands of people.

A Civilian on the Shuttle

The United States' National Aeronautics and Space Administration (NASA) is sensitive to the need to publicize the importance of its work for our understanding of the universe and for new products that have enriched our lives. Since it is dependent on Congress to provide funds for its budget, NASA must win approval from the public if it is to continue its work.

One way NASA sought to promote its work was to put a teacher in space. Christa McAuliffe won the competition to be the first ordinary citizen to fly on the shuttle. Although she died in the shuttle that exploded on takeoff, she did much in her life to emphasize the importance of "reaching for the stars." In the long run, it will be voters who determine whether cost will be a barrier to future flight.

Flying Through Tomorrow

Just as there was speculation about whether flight was possible beyond the speed of sound, now scientists argue about whether people will ever travel faster than the speed of light, which is 186,000 miles per second (299,460 kilometers per second). We will need to travel at high speeds to fly beyond our solar system.

If we can travel faster than the speed of light, we will enter the mystery of traveling faster than Earth time. Albert Einstein theorized that we live in a universe with four dimensions: length, width, height, and time. According to this great physicist, time is *relative*; it has to be measured by the movement of something in relation to something else, like the orbit of Earth relative to the Sun. If we could exceed the speed of light, we would go ahead of the light waves and pass the light waves that went out earlier, so we would appear to be going back in time. If we could do this, we could travel for many Earth years and come back younger than the people we'd left behind. However, Einstein also thought that the speed of light is as fast as anything with mass (such as our three-dimensional bodies) can go.

We do know of two subatomic particles that travel at the speed of light. Photons and neutrinos within an atom have no mass and therefore no resistance to traveling at the speed of light. As we learn more, we may figure out a way to travel as fast as we want.

AMAZING FACTS

Our nearest star is 4.3 years away if we could travel at the speed of light, but a trip across our Milky Way galaxy would take about 100,000 years at light speed.

AMAZING FACTS

If we were traveling faster than the speed of light and watched a clock mounted on a tower, the clock would seem to run backward like a videotape in reverse.

Christa McAuliffe (1948–1986)

When James Beggs, administrator of NASA, announced the selection of a teacher as the first private citizen to go up in the shuttle, he said, "This agency lives and dies by whether we can attract top talent and keep kids interested in the space program." Christa McAuliffe won the chance over 11,500 applicants to ride the space shuttle, *Challenger*. What made Christa McAuliffe so special?

She was the oldest child of Ed and Grace Corrigan, born in 1948 in Boston. Her father was a college student in an industrial management course, so her family was living on a very tight budget when she arrived. Four younger brothers and sisters were to join the family. As a child, she had problems with asthma and motion sickness.

Christa attended a Roman Catholic high school where she met her future husband, Steven James McAuliffe, when they were fifteen years old. They became engaged a year later but agreed to wait for marriage until they both had finished college. Christa said that her best preparation for the NASA contest was the Girl Scout competition in which she participated to go to the Roundup in Idaho.

Of average intelligence but an overachiever when it came to activities and schoolwork, Christa McAuliffe graduated from Framingham State College. After she married in 1970, she lived and taught in Maryland for a while, often accepting the challenge of working with the most difficult pupils. Her favorite teaching tool was the field trip. She pursued a masters degree at Bowie State College. At twenty-seven, she had her first child, a son, followed a few years later by her daughter.

The family moved to New Hampshire where she became a highly regarded teacher. In 1984, she heard about the Teacher in Space program, and she met the fairly simple requirements to enter. Space had always fascinated her. Still, she waited until the last day to mail her application, going over and over the essay that she had to write about why she wanted to enter the program.

From the pool of 11,500, 113 teachers were selected to go to Washington, D.C., for further interviews. From this number, 10 were chosen as finalists and sent to Houston for grueling psychological and physical tests. Christa was the one chosen go into space. Perhaps she had best grasped the importance of young people to the space program. "I want to show my students how the space program connects with them, how it belongs to them. If students don't see themselves as part of history, they don't really get involved. I want to bring them up in the space program, and maybe if they see me as part of history, it will help them share that with future generations."

When it was finally time for the launch in January of 1986, her plans for teaching in space were complete. One of the T-shirts that she was taking along with her had the slogan: "I touch the Future — I teach." Her family, her town, her fellow teachers, and the whole country watched with pride as she cheerfully waited out the delays of the launch. On the fateful day in below-freezing weather, the *Challenger* rose from the launch pad and then exploded, killing the crew of seven.

This ending taught a good deal about the importance of cold even on very small parts of an aircraft — such as an O-ring seal found to be a major cause of the explosion — about the decision-making process involved in launching, and about how an investigation can lead to improvements. Christa McAuliffe was not forgotten. Her willingness to "reach for the stars" is shared by many others.

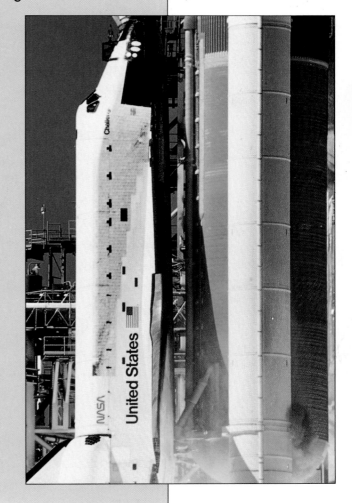

The ill-fated space shuttle Challenger *lifts off on January 28, 1986. The puff of black smoke at the base of the white solid rocket booster shows where an O-ring seal failed to work.*

Environmental Concerns Plague Air Travel

In the meantime, many worry that bigger SSTs may harm our atmosphere. At one time, scientists thought water vapor and carbon dioxide from SST engine exhaust would cause climate changes. Another theory was that the nitrous oxides from the exhaust would react with the ozone layer in the stratosphere and reduce the protection ozone provides from harmful ultraviolet sunlight. If our ozone layer goes, then damage to crops and an increase in skin cancers might result. A 1993 study showed that small increases of nitrous oxide actually seem to slow the destruction of ozone at lower stratosphere levels, where SSTs fly. However, scientists warn that if the exhaust rises to higher levels in the atmosphere, then ozone loss may increase. Newly designed engines show that the output of nitrous oxide can be cut, but clearly the SST will have to be monitored for safety to the environment.

This is especially important because NASA has a High Speed Civil Transport program and estimates that there will be thousands of SSTs in service by the year 2015. A European group has also announced that it is looking for a plane to follow the Concorde model.

We've already seen the problems of ground transportation in large cities, where vehicle exhaust pollutes the air and heavy traffic increases the risk of accidents. Some busy airports, such as Chicago's O'Hare and New York's La Guardia, frequently make pilots circle for fifteen to thirty minutes while they wait their turn for a clear runway — a sort of traffic jam in the sky. People who live under airspace around airports have already imposed limits on flight patterns in many communities. Will we see more restrictions in the future on who can fly and where they can fly? Air traffic control services are currently stretched to the point that accidents occur from control tower errors. In the future, we may need the air traffic equivalent of traffic lights in the sky to keep us from crashing into one another.

AMAZING FACTS

Wind tunnels have changed as much as aircraft since the Wright brothers used the crude wooden one they built to test their planes. Now, wind tunnels can create wind velocities at twenty times the speed of sound (Mach 20) and operate at temperatures that range between thousands of degrees above zero to hundreds of degrees below. The world's largest wind tunnel is at NASA's Ames Research Center.

In 1990, NASA found that there is widespread space "junk" in an orbit between 530 miles (850 kilometers) to 620 miles (1,000 kilometers) above Earth, a region already crowded with satellites. Much of this is from old nuclear-powered satellites that are leaking radioactive debris. Aside from the obvious dangers of radioactivity, this debris can move at such fast speeds that it can hit and damage satellites or anything else flying through this area. Scientists are now trying to shield future satellites from this new danger. Space, which once seemed so huge, is quickly becoming crowded, at least in the space "neighborhood" of Earth.

While we still have many problems to overcome, we can gain hope when we consider how far we've traveled in a short period of time. General Charles E. Yeager summarized our progress: "It is intellectually staggering to note that only during this century has man acquired the basic knowledge permitting him to fly; and in the relatively minute time period of three-quarters-of-a-century, has taken this knowledge and expanded it from wood and fabric biplanes capable of just over 12 miles per hour, to 2,500 ton space shuttles and lunar exploration rockets capable of accelerating immense manned vehicles to orbital speeds and beyond. It's a marvelous and seemingly incomprehensible contrast, indeed."

The Pathfinder solar-powered aircraft is tested in October 1993. It is an unpiloted, all-wing plane, powered by eight electric motors that drive propellers. The power comes from solar cells on the upper surface of the wing, supplemented by batteries.

Timeline

1500 — Leonardo da Vinci draws ideas for a person in flight.

1709 — Bartolomeu de Gusamo demonstrates an unpiloted hot air balloon for King John V of Portugal.

1903 — The Wright brothers make successful controlled, powered flights in *The Flyer* at Kitty Hawk, North Carolina.

1906 — Alberto Santos-Dumont flies his biplane at 25.65 miles per hour (41.3 kilometers per hour).

1909 — Louis Blériot flies the *Blériot XI*, a monoplane, from Calais, France, to Dover, England.

1914 — World War I begins, during which experiments in aviation go forward.

1918 — Airmail service begins between Washington, D.C., and New York City.

1927 — Charles Lindbergh completes a solo, nonstop flight in the *Spirit of St. Louis* from New York to Paris, France.

1932 — Amelia Earhart flies from Newfoundland, Canada, to Ireland.

1936 — The Douglas DC-3 passenger plane begins service in the United States.

1939 — World War II begins with Germany sending its air force to attack Poland, France, and Britain.

1939 — Igor Sikorsky flies a successful model of a helicopter.

1941 — Frank Whittle tests the first successful jet-powered flight.

1945 — The B-29 Superfortress *Enola Gay* drops the atom bomb on Japan, thereby ending World War II.

1947 — General Charles Yeager breaks the sound barrier in the X-1, *Glamorous Glennis*.

1968–9 — Soviet and British-French models of supersonic transport planes fly.

1982 — The shuttle completes its first mission, reaching a speed of Mach 25.

1986 — Dick Rutan and Jeanna Yeager fly nonstop around the world without refueling in the *Voyager*, a plane designed by Burt Rutan.

1991 — Desert Storm of the Persian Gulf War demonstrates the importance of air supremacy with the introduction of many new types of planes.

Further Reading

Aaseng, Nathan. *Breaking the Sound Barrier.* New York: Julian Messner, 1991.

Boyne, Walter J. *The Smithsonian Book of Flight for Young People.* New York: Atheneum, 1988.

Briggs, Carole. *At the Controls: Women in Aviation.* Minneapolis: Lerner Publications, 1991.

Bringhurst, John. *Planes, Jets, and Helicopters: Great Paper Airplanes.* Blue Ridge Summit, PA: McGraw-Hill, 1994.

Jefferis, David. *Supersonic Flight: New Frontiers of Aviation.* New York: Franklin Watts, 1988.

Lomax, Judy. *Women of the Air.* New York: Dodd, Mead & Company, 1987.

Phelps, J. Alfred. *They Had a Dream: The Story of African-American Astronauts.* Novato, CA: Presidio Press, 1994.

Stacey, Thomas. *Airplanes: The Lure of Flight.* San Diego: Lucent Books, 1990.

Sullivan, George. *They Flew Alone.* New York: Frederick Warne & Company, 1969.

Walker, Ormiston H. *Experimenting with Air and Flight.* New York: Franklin Watts, 1989.

Glossary

Aerodynamics: The science of the motion of gases (including air) and of the forces acting on objects when they move through gases.

Buffeting: The beating of an object or a surface by an unsteady flow, such as gusts. Also, an irregular shaking of an object because of turbulent air or separated flow.

Compressibility: The characteristic of a substance like air by which its density increases with increases in pressure. In air, this happens at high speeds such as that around the speed of sound.

Drag: A slowing force that acts on an object in motion through air or other gases.

Hypersonic: Pertaining to speeds of Mach 5.0 or greater.

Lift: The force acting upward on an object created by a change in air pressure as it moves around the object.

Machmeter: The instrument that measures and indicates speed in relation to the speed of sound. It tells the Mach number.

Mach number: A number that gives the ratio of the speed of an object in relation to the speed of sound in the surrounding medium, such as air.

Pitch: A movement up or down.

Sonic: Pertaining to the speed of sound.

Sonic boom: A sound like an explosion that is heard when a shock wave from an aircraft flying at supersonic speed reaches the ear.

Stratosphere: One of several upper layers of the atmosphere.

Subsonic: Pertaining to speeds less than the speed of sound.

Supersonic: Pertaining to speeds greater than the speed of sound.

Thrust: The pushing or pulling force developed by an aircraft or rocket engine.

Transonic: Pertaining to what occurs within the speed range where flow patterns change from subsonic to supersonic or supersonic to subsonic, about Mach 0.8 to Mach 1.2.

Wind tunnel: A tubelike structure in which a high-speed movement of air or gas is produced, used to test the airflow around airplanes.

Yaw: A side-to-side movement.

Index

Numbers in *italic* indicate pictures; numbers in **bold** indicate biographies